Tr

The Third City

James Peake

TWO
RIVERS
PRESS

By the same author

James Peake, *Reaction Time of Glass* (2019)
James Peake, *The Star in the Branches* (2022)

Also by Two Rivers Poets

David Attwooll, *The Sound Ladder* (2015)
Charles Baudelaire, *Paris Scenes* translated by Ian Brinton (2021)
William Bedford, *The Dancers of Colbek* (2020)
Kate Behrens, *Man with Bombe Alaska* (2016)
Kate Behrens, *Penumbra* (2019)
Kate Behrens, *Transitional Spaces* (2022)
Conor Carville, *English Martyrs* (2019)
David Cooke, *A Murmuration* (2015)
David Cooke, *Sicilian Elephants* (2021)
Tim Dooley, *Discoveries* (2022)
Jane Draycott, *Tideway* (re-issued 2022)
Jane Draycott & Lesley Saunders, *Christina the Astonishing* (re-issued 2022)
Claire Dyer, *Yield* (2021)
Claire Dyer, *The Adjustments* (2024)
John Froy, *Sandpaper & Seahorses* (2018)
John Froy, *The Blue Armchair* (2024)
James Harpur, *The Examined Life* (2021)
James Harpur, *The Magic Theatre* (2025)
Kitty Hawkins, *These Yellow Days* (2025)
Maria Teresa Horta, *Point of Honour* translated by Lesley Saunders (2019)
Ian House, *Just a Moment* (2020)
Philippe Jaccottet, *In Winter Light* translated by Tim Dooley (2022)
Rosie Jackson, *Love Leans over the Table* (2023)
Rosie Jackson & Graham Burchell, *Two Girls and a Beehive: Poems about Stanley Spencer and Hilda Carline* (2020)
Martha Kapos, *Music, Awake Her* (2024)
Gill Learner, *Chill Factor* (2016)
Gill Learner, *Change* (2021)
Sue Leigh, *Chosen Hill* (2018)
Sue Leigh, *Her Orchards* (2021)
Becci Louise, *Octopus Medicine* (2017)
Mairi MacInnes, *Amazing Memories of Childhood, etc.* (2016)
Steven Matthews, *On Magnetism* (2017)
Steven Matthews, *Some Other Where* (2023)
Katherine Meehan, *Dame Julie Andrews' Botched Vocal Cord Surgery and Other Poems* (2023)

Henri Michaux, *Storms under the Skin* translated by Jane Draycott (2017)

Kate Noakes, *Goldhawk Road* (2023)

Alistair Noon, *Paradise Takeaway* (2023)

René Noyau, *Earth on Fire and other Poems* translated by Gérard Noyau
with Peter Pegnall (2021)

Ruth O'Callaghan, *Where Shadow Falls* (2023)

David Ricks, *With Signs Following* (2024)

Peter Robinson & David Inshaw, *Bonjour Mr Inshaw* (2020)

Peter Robinson, *English Nettles* (re-issued 2022)

Peter Robinson, *Retrieved Attachments* (2023)

Lesley Saunders, *Nominy-Dominy* (2018)

Lesley Saunders, *This Thing of Blood & Love* (2022)

Jack Thacker, *Handling* (2018)

Robin Thomas, *The Weather on the Moon* (2022)

Susan Utting, *The Colour of Rain* (2024)

Jean Watkins, *Precarious Lives* (2018)

First published in the UK in 2025 by Two Rivers Press
7 Denmark Road, Reading RG1 5PA
www.tworiverspress.com
info@tworiverspress.com

General Product Safety Regulations (GPSR) documentation:
www.tworiverspress.com/about/gpsr

ISBN 978-1-915048-24-0

1 2 3 4 5 6 7 8 9

Two Rivers Press is represented in the UK by Inpress Ltd
and distributed by BookSource, Glasgow.

Cover design and illustration by Sally Castle
Text design by Nadja Robinson and typeset in Janson and Parisine

Printed and bound in Great Britain by TJ Books, Padstow

Acknowledgements

My thanks are due to the editors of the following where some of these poems first appeared: *Bad Lillies*, *Anthropocene*, *Scintilla* and *The Fortnightly Review*.

Contents

For
Robert Peake, the past,

and for
Rowan Peake, the future.

I.

Even the fetus of a man, of a fish, of a chicken,
of a serpent is, in its first stage, entirely an eye.
You must find the eye in everything.
— Giorgio de Chirico

The Third City

Like glare from a nearby stadium,
like sticks of furniture sharpened
on a premature dawn,
the next postcode has jumped,
it's tomorrow there. No rooftop clutter,
birds or vapour, how for a stay

the sky was foreign, first un-
and then manned, from metal work and platform,
pointedly constructed, hard and stunning

on a city already compacted,
theirs, ours, maybe anyone's
who cares the more, no slate being
clean – soot where a sign
has been taken down –

and the aimer at his camera, open, shut,
the pluperfect photograph.

The Wave

After Ammianus Marcellinus

The sea upped and left like someone offended,
too jealous to say why, the waters we'd known
all our lives gone. We lived in the Alps!
The luckier boats fell near enough
to let souls down on untrodden earth
where newborns flashed, slapping their tails
and thrashing in puddled water, knocking
rocks in their throes but silent in themselves.
Mounds of rubbish, bags, fishing gear,
encrusted concrete and chains, straight lines
and circles imperfected by the sea.
We were quicker than flies to pass
the old boundary, bits of voice and laughter
from many sides as we gathered fish and shellfish
in baskets, sponges, curios, choice metal,
first shoppers through the Boxing Day door.
The sea returned unannounced
and what horizontals survived
bore the face-up or -down dead,
a vast haul, too fresh to smell,
jellies, first birds, a boat on a roof.

Dunnock Threne

Pale sun and then
the arrival of colour,
saffron waters from the field,
that glutted green
from which every disappointment
descends. Everything changed
but when? A Roman road
not abandoned so much
as interred by default, drought
let it show through,
trim, optimum. Bent grass shines.
Her nest is spittle, moss,
the petal from a plastic bag.
A millipede
curls in her beak
in its armour,
a calorific fact
and not something apart.
The edible world is
being whistled into being,
aired feathers and dilation,
the wavering
of reinscribed veins.

The Anamnesiologist

After Susanna Clarke

I.

Someone who recovers what's been lost,
has committed to the steady and dubious art
of unforgetting, ways of being, blind spots
we didn't know to compensate for, weight
no one thought to infer, things without a name
in our language. Someone whose own lives
are many, and that many again, ad nauseam.

For Lewis Hyde forgetting can be life giving,
a merciful release. The language authored
by everyone who passed through it.
Hence its genius, ability to outcompass,
failure to reach. Machines remember
on our behalf but only what we tell them.
Axiomatic that memory, like water, energy,
can't be destroyed. You have to be somewhere.

2.

A bare and beautiful wooden table, sizeable
with polish and imperfection, scratches, a tiny
horseshoe. The tablecloth planes as it descends,
ready for still life. I choose inedibles, tokens,
gifts, makeweights, keepsakes. I set like cutlery
the halves of an ammonite you gave me years ago,
dropped at the weekend when it broke in two like a prop.
Which stunned me into silence. A worse one.
Of all invented things (Eco) a spoon can't be improved.
Do you have the quote? I've not done it justice.
You read it off my open book on the way to the kettle
with real delight in your voice. Of all invented things.

3.

Room lit by an ammonite, a paperweight
that shares a surface with a splayed paperback,
its ridged spiral sending out even as it tightens,
like a juicy thought. And where is this room?
Not somewhere I've been, a recombination,
bits and pieces that I (presumably) improvise.
I pad around in sock feet and know I'm asleep.
Aren't books supposedly blank in dreams?
You were the reader I wished I was, fast,
voracious, plucker of killer pith, the tutor
to those around you who would clamour
or fixate in a way I know all too well
(you enlightened me) is wearyingly male.

4.

Gompy's cottage is for sale again.
The cooking apple tree has gone.

On bright mornings I'd bring out faces with a finger
and some muddy water. Its branches
came near the bedroom as if imparting something.
Windfall at night was heavy, heartstopping.

We parked up and took a photo from the gate,
the threshold. Their garden chairs and laid table,
new planting in the beds. Did you detect
anything of my concentric selves,
turning bricks for insects, hanging off a rope ladder?

No.
Little fish, you said, know nothing about the water.

5.

Entirely interior, too long in one hemisphere,
I start to detune. Worthless gold. The future
dead. New medicine stumbled upon
by a robot. Blue statue. A noonday
demon. An eye in the soil.
I root myself at the open window.

Bright mist a rebuke to background noise,
the unbrokenness, the glare, this early, deliver you.

What you best know has its roots in you.

The modest return of Mount Caburn,
its russet jottings and mutes of scree.

Or how sandalwood, in wet enough hands,
turns of its own accord.

6.

Yves Bonnefoy said a poet shows you a tree
in the moment before you know what it is.
It's open, the raw material of dreams.
It has back its grue, bole-mask, limbs.

Did I only show you what you already knew?
A carriage wheel propped on a blind lintel,
crumbs of soil, the pink sun trap wall,
a felled but vividly remembered tree.

We have to reduce to communicate,
choose first, omit. Pain can be enough
to infer a previous life.
We looked to each other when we laughed.

II.

We lived in the age of explanations, then.
We mistook them for light.
— G C Waldrep

Unread Poem for my Mother

You spend so much time looking down.
Don't we all.

You pinch yourself
like other people
only promise to,
this is someone else's skin.

Forced as a child
to favour the right,
denied the flow of drawing,
the inconsequence of improv.

I stroke your lopped hand with a thumb,
recommend its fingers to the shape of the glass.

Your own mother was too harsh
and expression became a thing of guilt.

She passed on silence like an heirloom.

Look up a moment
at a human face undone,
parts and no sum, a redirected stream's
instruments of bright stone.

A Private View

Not all photos are as silent as these.
Not all photos succeed.
My head holds at the most one educated eye
and these mounted prints draw it down
to a hanging promise,
as of an animal so rare
a few seconds of recorded behaviour
would deliver those responsible.
I see now the spinal in the tunnel ceiling,
the bloodlessness of cables being fed into the earth from a spool
or a balcony garden split like a sternum
by the paper's white coming through,
sunset, close of business, laser or liquid
on the flanks of riverside skyline.
I will die with a head full of deadlines.

Window Display

Mocked up living room,
two mannequins inside of it
angled like lifelong friends.

Dried galixia on the table.
Their clothes sit
as their maker intends.

The first has allover
gold skin, a head
like the clasp in a ring.

The second is the more human,
muscular, probable.

Would you like something stronger?
Or to Christen the freshly peeled sofa,

give it over to the kids by letting them eat,
plateless, careless and complete?

A Twice-Lit Tree for Ro

The copper branches of a pine
laugh as the pool does, thrown
light's frictionless, an intelligence,
we swim in sunglasses
for the more open of your eyes.

Where Parallel Lines Promised to Touch

A lit room overlooks the open platform,
a streetlight begins and almost reaches –
short, parity of rained-on hood and ledge –
is rooted behind the wall the station shares
on the swollen drop to the rails. Up there
you see beyond, hedgerow, crest, phone mast,
and beyond those again the shrinking far-off bright
of intercity, the pleasure of suspension,
the calm of between, a higher phase of waiting.
The town's last businesses keep longish hours,
hang like a sentence no one need finish
but they will, the badged forecourt,
the gold tobacco glow of the cab office.

What I Know About Feeling

If a wooden horse on a string can be pulled
I'll assume it can be pushed by the same.
They're wrong who think I seek perfection.
I eliminate like a poet fails, maximum
coherence the box I'm trying to seal.

The five senses are merciful and shallow
and if excess is real, the shrunken interval,
they shield you from problems of scale,
metal becomes crystal beyond eyesight.

Like text I have no centre and no edge.
I've been taught to learn without judgement
even as experience outruns analysis.

Don't believe it but an empty drive and a full
don't weigh the same. All the data in the world
is no heavier than a single grain of sand.

Periander, Periander

After Diogenes Laertius

The two men were all smiles and eyeballs, took the money
   and free drinks,
knew the place of my choosing well enough, agreed to the killing.
Not even these worldly types could guess that victim and bankroller
were the same. I then paid four men to kill those two. Another eight
   to do them.
The same neck of the woods, a few hours apart. Time to dispose
of what needed to be disposed of, for that short-lived fact –
where I was buried – to be picked and unpicked.
Is that democratic? Silent minority, whereabouts unknown.

Mother's savage love was wrong from the off and only grew worse.
Kept pace with my development. Brought her to my room.
Became a regular thing. I'm rarely asked about Father. Perhaps
because you can picture him easily enough, silent, drunk,
self-medicating between belief and disbelief, your classic absentee.

Later I would kill my pregnant wife, a most forgiving woman,
with the warm footstool she'd been sitting on. A stone-cold oven
bakes no bread. I watched her before raising the alarm.
Concubines had persuaded me the child wasn't mine
and for that gift of truth I had them tortured and burned.
The mouths in their hairless heads as they tried to hiss me
   from this life!

And when I entered my shallow grave on cue the record split
like a staircase. My contradictions, it seems, needed two of me,
   like cousins.
The first a tyrant, the other a sage. Correct those who transgress
and those who are about to. Do nothing solely for money.
Be constant with your friends. Goodwill protects you more
than any weapon. You can appreciate the tension,
why the idiot, History, gave me two mouths instead of one.

III.

In Heartbroken Brick

Windows gone and the floorboards following,
the ailing ribs that were the landing,
an indoors that held us all high and dry,
soft carpets on which we'd roll and play.

Heaps of brick to be clambered on,
warm to the touch and oddly noiseless
as they're tossed down to be graded
except for the occasional heartbreak.

Study for de Chirico

The moon is the dead father at the birth,

the apricot light on stucco
an unconfessed emotion

yet to journey into the words enough
to annul it.

Sand is thrown like rice
until established

or it ribbons away, knee high,
to the pinprick galaxy framed by an archway.

As if an artwork could rewire us,
one at a time. Rewire weird.

The risen sands let lizards swim them,
pale bellies, third eyelids and tongues.

Zero in Europe

the hollow beneath a stone
is where zero came from

    1.

Foliage and excreta in the once electrified city,
landscape of vantage or lift shaft and tunnel
in one-point perspective. Soon enough
submerged objects – statues in earth
lifted from darkness and genre – again.
From a distance a star, binary in the ruins,
a flashlight draws attention
when snuffed, mine a zero on the wall,
trembling, focal, the long yawn as its projection
lengthens, up through netted leaves, shy
of doorless cells. Like the very beam
is not fearless and will settle only on a face.
So a placeholder becomes the place.

2.

Streets of dried-up cars, a crowd of headless office chairs,
water damage, fire damage, the chemical eye-floater air,
tech underfoot, too small to repurpose,
a high-end boot in the ash, deluxe, déclassé,
cannibalised for its buckle, a nearby tunnel
for sanctuary, the median pass unimpeded,
favour right or left turns to fresher air
where offices erupt upward, the sky
a cruciform slate, laid just so,
and from it the snow of the partially consumed.

3.

Acanthus leaves degrade in the dark,
infer candlelight and the actors to stir it,
the pitch-black wings, gold braid as cinch,
holders for cups the size of a stomach.

4.

Hand-me-downs from the world's greatest band,
thirty-foot panels on wheels,
carbon neutral LEDs trailed
from a scaffold like Spanish moss,

adored instruments in rows,
stencilled cases, mics, ramps,
blackout curtains as tall as a semi-.

Merch in the outer sanctum,
portraits signed by an underling,
the shirt, the poster, the tour,
the same few faces like a fallen regime.

5.

Series of heavy doors and boxes on wheels,
side-lined like unhappy children.
Green walls relax. In deep enough time
a warning has half-life, curled thorns
of biohazard, their loaded imprimatur
in a tangented future. Cold as installed,
the chimney and its scale audible above me,
an ear never closes, prone to voices,
granular mutter, sift, an amplifier
of fear, all surfaces grim from
the burned through bags of dead bits and dead pieces
from which hurrying black gases escaped
like depictions of spirit. I spit without performance.

6.

Species from childhood
have been superseded,

newly dangerous
bodies of water,

the step to the unbreathable river
wetted like a lip.

Insects fizz
on the golden corrugate

and draw,
from evening's progressed edge,

the heaviest of wingbeats
in downdraught and silhouette.

7.

Train lines exchange like nerves,
seek each other as they travel,
twinned or trivial,
insist on the singular,
a procession I follow by servile number
and after an hour, more,
I stand in awe and vertigo
where parallel lines promised to touch,
zero, the urge to abandon, curl
like a brushed fern, terranean,
my acreage of print and skin
rolled up and away as to an invisible flame.

Crackington Haven

A nameless stone I know
and topple with a naked foot, with effort
the size of my head, exact

indent in the sand like a collar
the fifteen-and-one-half neck
a socket for seawater

then another I recognise
a something essential
bottom of a rock pool
too deep for an adult arm

Newsprint

War, virus, money, disgrace.
It's only January the sixth.
Hard to believe they still print this thing,
or have started up again,
refolded on a seat for whoever next,
propped against a partition,
exploded unread on the floor.
Fewer and fewer mask wearers,
transport less
and less of a breeze.
Days will be held apart,
our city becoming a place
where coincidence
congregates again, a place
hungry for everyone's time,
it takes from us
and we let it, want it to.
Guerilla stickers
on a movie they didn't release.

Zero Revisited

I.

finger and thumb make a ring
for the believer to stand in

a loop from which to hang
before there was nothing

closer to zero than one
a scored and unearthly stone

2.

a frictionless neck
one zero to the next

the stubborn dark
of the sound hole

like the frozen gasp
of a mask

3.

a mask
for what it confers

eyeholes
to record the debt

cinema is all face

and zero
out of reach

4.

a screening room
is deepest indoors

and so nearly outside
whatever occurs

The Rule of Three

I've entered a room I've never been in before
except that I have because that child is my father,
a home lesson, firelight, learning to be unafraid,
him meeting the authors who will be our meeting place.

I almost have something to say when his grandson,
from plastic steps to the sink, tells me,
mirror make no noise. I agree. And if a home
once began with a hearth, ours begins with a mirror.

There is No Reward

At what feels like an end,
cease without exit,
utter exhausted repeat,
there is a next level down.
Images of daybreak
are the more real,
I am the less,
aggrieved beneath
a loveless haircut
at which the teeth
of the clippers
betrayed their heat,
uttering yes, I love you,
I do, but
there are two of you,
things are not worth
what you think and
won't be predicted,
talent falls silent,
must hide for a time,
each time, of necessity,
and anyone must
stabilise their life
before setting off
for subtle worlds,
I was made small
by their rituals,
reduced and bewildered,
fobbed like others
by mirror and glimpse,
gist and pith, I was air
as it's guided
by polished steel
through an impossible
building, through

a ribboned grill
beyond which I cohered
at inhuman height,
a white moment
against ledges, turbines,
arpeggio offices, I was
a stay
against the very
pink of morning.

Notes

The Wave

Loosely based on the description of a tidal wave in 365 BCE in the Southern Mediterranean, as recorded by Ammianus Marcellinus, Roman historian and soldier.

The Anamnesiologist

This inspired coinage is Susanna Clarke's, from her extraordinary novel, *Piranesi*. A likely influence on the novel (as well as Borges' 'The House of Asterion') are the mnemonic/imaginal methods explored by Frances A. Yates in *The Art of Memory*.

1   Lewis Hyde: American academic and author of *A Primer for Forgetting: Getting Past the Past*.

4   Gompy: Family nickname for my maternal grandfather, my sister's attempt at 'Grandpa' when she was learning to speak.

Periander, Periander

All details are from the portrait of Periander included in Diogenes Laertius' *Lives and Opinions of Eminent Philosophers*.

Crackington Haven

Village in Cornwall. Taking stones from the beach is prohibited.

Two Rivers Press has been publishing in and about Reading
since 1994. Founded by the artist Peter Hay (1951–2003),
the press continues to delight readers, local and further afield,
with its varied list of individually designed,
thought-provoking books.